THE REVISED CATECHISM

NOTE

The Revised Catechism was drawn up by the Archbishops' Commission to Revise the Church Catechism. It was commended for use in teaching first by the Convocations of Canterbury and York and since 1973 by the General Synod of the Church of England. The most recent extension of the period of commendation is from 1 January 1996 until discontinued by resolution of the Synod.

First published in Great Britain in 1962

Society for Promoting Christian Knowledge
36 Causton Street
London SW1P 4ST

British Library Cataloguing-in-Publication Data
A catalogue record for this book is available from the British Library.

ISBN-13: 978–0–281–05904–1
ISBN-10: 0–281–05904–7

10 9 8 7 6 5 4 3 2 1

First printed in Great Britain by Hart-Talbot Ltd, Saffron Walden.
Reprinted in Great Britain by Ashford Colour Press.

Preface to the 1996 edition by the Archbishop of York

'Forward with Basics!' is a fair alternative title to the Revised Catechism. For the definite basics of the Faith are to be found here, expressed in terse question and answer form, which Anglicans have found of value for over four decades.

During that time interrogative forms of teaching have gone out of fashion, only to return, vying with a philosophy of 'finding out for oneself' rather than learning by rote. Both/and rather than either/or seems the best solution to these alternative approaches. For whilst working out the implications of one's faith from first principles is a laudable aim, having an armoury of over fifty specimen questions and answers can only aid the way one presents that faith to a thirsty world.

The original work was written in an age oblivious to the need for inclusive language, so please treat it tolerantly and transpose accordingly. For the basics of Anglican doctrine are well represented here. Most of the questions and answers themselves contain key words which signal the need for further investigation and discussion. This is all to the good, since the Catechism aims to whet the appetite rather than provide a complete meal.

That being said, some of these appetizers could not be bettered by the most magnificent theological feast. For instance the final paragraph on Christian assurance, rich in Pauline imagery, is as eloquent as it is succinct. Were Anglicans able to fire the whole of their faith and witness with such good examples set in this work, then the task of Evangelism, to which we are all called, would make a major advance. To that worthy end I commend this new edition wholeheartedly.

The Revised Catechism

I. THE CALL OF GOD: THE CHRISTIAN ANSWER

1 **What is your Christian name?**
My Christian name is ....

2 **Who gave you this name?**
My parents and godparents gave me this name at my Baptism.

3 **What did God do for you in your Baptism?**
In my Baptism God called me to himself, and I was made a member of Christ, the child of God, and an inheritor of the kingdom of heaven.

4 **What did your godparents promise for you at your Baptism?**
At my Baptism my godparents made three promises to God for me: first, that I would renounce the devil and fight against evil; secondly, that I would hold fast the Christian Faith and put my whole trust in Christ as Lord and Saviour; thirdly, that I would obediently keep God's holy will and commandments and serve him faithfully all the days of my life.

5 **Are you bound to do as they promised?**
Yes, certainly, and by God's help I will.

II. CHRISTIAN BELIEF

6 **Where do you find a summary of this Christian Faith which you are bound to believe and hold fast?**
I find a summary of the Christian Faith in the Apostles' Creed and in the Nicene Creed.

7 **Repeat the Apostles' Creed.**
I believe in God the Father Almighty, maker of heaven and earth:

And in Jesus Christ his only Son our Lord, who was conceived by the Holy Ghost, born of the Virgin Mary, suffered under Pontius Pilate, was crucified, dead, and buried, he descended into hell; the third day he rose again from the dead, he ascended into heaven, and sitteth on the right hand of God the Father Almighty; from thence he shall come to judge the quick and the dead.

I believe in the Holy Ghost; the holy catholic Church; the communion of saints; the forgiveness of sins; the resurrection of the body, and the life everlasting. Amen.

8 **What do you learn from the Creeds?**
From the Creeds I learn to believe in one God, Father, Son, and Holy Ghost, who is the creator and ruler of the universe, and has made all things for his glory.

9 **What does the Church teach about God the Father?**
The Church teaches that God the Father made me and all mankind, and that in his love he sent his Son to reconcile the world to himself.

10 **What does the Church teach about God the Son?**
The Church teaches that, for our salvation, God the Son became man and died for our sins; that he was raised victorious over death and was exalted to the throne of God as our advocate and intercessor; and that he will come as our judge and saviour.

11 **What does the Church teach about God the Holy Spirit?**
The Church teaches that God the Holy Spirit inspires all that is good in mankind; that he came in his fulness at Pentecost to be the giver of life in the Church, and that he enables me to grow in likeness to Jesus Christ.

Thus I learn to believe in one God, Father, Son, and Holy Spirit, and this Holy Trinity I praise and magnify saying:

Glory be to the Father, and to the Son, and to the Holy Ghost: as it was in the beginning, is now, and ever shall be, world without end. Amen.

III. THE CHURCH AND MINISTRY

12 **What is the Church?**
The Church is the family of God and the Body of Christ through which he continues his reconciling work among men. Its members on earth enter it by baptism and are one company with those who worship God in heaven.

13 **How is the Church described in the Creeds?**
The Church is described as One, Holy, Catholic, and Apostolic.

14 **What do you mean by these words?**
By these words I mean that:

the Church is *One* because, in spite of its divisions, it is one family under one Father, whose purpose is to unite all men in Jesus Christ our Lord;

the Church is *Holy* because it is set apart by God for himself, through the Holy Spirit;

the Church is *Catholic* because it is universal, for all nations and for all time, holding the Christian Faith in its fulness;

the Church is *Apostolic* because it is sent to preach the Gospel to the whole world, and receives its divine authority and teaching from Christ through his Apostles.

15 **What orders of ministers are there in the Church?**
There are these orders of ministers in the Church: Bishops, Priests, and Deacons.

16 **What is the work of a Bishop?**
The work of a Bishop is to be a chief shepherd and a ruler in the Church; to guard the Faith; to ordain and confirm; and to be the chief minister of the Word and Sacraments in his diocese.

17 **What is the work of a Priest?**
The work of a Priest is to preach the word of God, to teach, and to baptize; to celebrate the Holy Communion;

to pronounce absolution and blessing in God's name; and to care for the people entrusted by the Bishop to his charge.

18 **What is the work of a Deacon?**
The work of a Deacon is to help the Priest both in the conduct of worship and in the care of souls.

19 **What is the Church of England?**
The Church of England is the ancient Church of this land, catholic and reformed. It proclaims and holds fast the doctrine and ministry of the One, Holy, Catholic, and Apostolic Church.

20 **What is the Anglican Communion?**
The Anglican Communion is a family of Churches within the universal Church of Christ, maintaining apostolic doctrine and order and in full communion with one another and with the Sees of Canterbury and York.

IV. CHRISTIAN OBEDIENCE

21 **The third promise made at your Baptism binds you to keep God's commandments all the days of your life. Where has God made these commandments known?**
God has made his commandments known in the Scriptures of the Old and New Testaments, especially in the teaching and example of our Lord Jesus Christ.

22 **Repeat the ten commandments found in the law of Moses.**

1 I am the Lord thy God who brought thee out of the land of Egypt, out of the house of bondage. Thou shalt have none other gods but me.

2 Thou shalt not make to thyself any graven image, nor the likeness of anything that is in heaven above, or in the earth beneath, or in the water under the earth. Thou shalt not bow down to them nor worship them.

3 Thou shalt not take the name of the Lord thy God in vain.
4 Remember that thou keep holy the Sabbath day. Six days shalt thou labour and do all that thou hast to do; but the seventh day is the Sabbath of the Lord thy God.
5 Honour thy father and thy mother.
6 Thou shalt do no murder.
7 Thou shalt not commit adultery.
8 Thou shalt not steal.
9 Thou shalt not bear false witness against thy neighbour.
10 Thou shalt not covet.

23 **Repeat the words of our Lord Jesus Christ about God's commandments.**
Our Lord Jesus Christ said: 'Thou shalt love the Lord thy God with all thy heart, and with all thy soul, and with all thy mind, and with all thy strength. This is the first commandment. And the second is like, namely this: Thou shalt love thy neighbour as thyself.' Again: 'A new commandment I give unto you, that ye love one another as I have loved you.'

24 **What then is your duty towards God?**
My duty towards God is:

1 to worship him as the only true God, to love, trust, and obey him, and by witness of my words and deeds to bring others to serve him;
2 to allow no created thing to take his place, but to use my time, my gifts, and my possessions as one who must give an account to him;
3 to reverence him in thought, word, and deed;
4 to keep the Lord's day for worship, prayer, and rest from work.

25 **What is your duty towards your neighbour?**
My duty towards my neighbour is:

5 to love, respect, and help my parents; to honour the

Queen; to obey those in authority over me in all things lawful and good; and to fulfil my duties as a citizen;

6 to hurt nobody by word or deed; to bear no grudge or hatred in my heart; to promote peace among men; to be courteous to all; and to be kind to all God's creatures;

7 to be clean in thought, word, and deed, controlling my bodily desires through the power of the Holy Spirit who dwells within me; and if called to the state of marriage to live faithfully in it;

8 to be honest and fair in all I do; not to steal or cheat; to seek justice, freedom, and plenty for all men;

9 to keep my tongue from lying, slandering, and harmful gossip, and never by my silence to let others be wrongly condemned;

10 to be thankful and generous; to do my duty cheerfully, and not to be greedy or envious.

Thus I acknowledge God's reign among men and try to live as a citizen of his kingdom, fighting against evil wherever I find it, in myself, or in the world around me.

V. THE HOLY SPIRIT IN THE CHURCH

Grace

26 **How can you carry out these duties and overcome temptation and sin?**
I can do these things only by the help of God and through his grace.

27 **What do you mean by God's grace?**
By God's grace I mean that God himself acts in Jesus Christ to forgive, inspire, and strengthen me by his Holy Spirit.

28 **In what ways do you receive these gifts of God's grace?**
I receive these gifts of God's grace within the fellowship of the Church, when I worship and pray, when I read the Bible, when I receive the Sacraments, and as I live my daily life to his glory.

Worship and Prayer

29 **What do you mean by the worship of God?**
To worship God is to respond to his love, first by joining in the Church's offering of praise, thanksgiving, and prayer, and by hearing his holy word; secondly by acknowledging him as the Lord of my life, and by doing my work for his honour and glory.

30 **Why do we keep Sunday as the chief day of public worship?**
We keep Sunday as the chief day of public worship because it was on the first day of the week that our Lord Jesus Christ rose from the dead.

31 **What is prayer?**
Prayer is the lifting up of heart and mind to God. We adore him, we confess our sins and ask to be forgiven, we thank him, we pray for others and for ourselves, we listen to him and seek to know his will.

32 **Repeat the Lord's Prayer.**
Our Father, which art in heaven, hallowed be thy name, thy kingdom come, thy will be done, in earth as it is in heaven. Give us this day our daily bread; and forgive us our trespasses, as we forgive them that trespass against us; and lead us not into temptation, but deliver us from evil. For thine is the kingdom, the power, and the glory, for ever and ever. Amen.

The Bible

33 **What is the Bible?**
The Bible, in both the Old and the New Testaments, is the record of God's revelation of himself to mankind through his people Israel, and above all in his Son, Jesus Christ.

34 **How was the Bible given to us?**
The Bible was given to us by the Holy Spirit who first inspired and guided the writers, and then led the Church to accept their writings as Holy Scripture.

35 **How should we read the Bible?**
We should read the Bible with the desire and prayer that through it God will speak to us by his Holy Spirit, and enable us to know him and do his will.

The Gospel Sacraments and other Ministries of Grace

36 **What do you mean by a sacrament?**
By a sacrament I mean the use of material things as signs and pledges of God's grace, and as a means by which we receive his gifts.

37 **What are the two parts of a sacrament?**
The two parts of a sacrament are the outward and visible sign, and the inward and spiritual grace.

38 **How many sacraments has Christ, in the Gospel, appointed for his Church?**
Christ in the Gospel has appointed two sacraments for his Church, as needed by all for fulness of life, Baptism, and Holy Communion.

39 **What other sacramental ministries of grace are provided in the Church?**
Other sacramental ministries of grace are confirmation, ordination, holy matrimony, the ministry of absolution, and the ministry of healing.

40 **What is *Baptism*?**
Baptism is the sacrament in which, through the action of the Holy Spirit, we are 'christened' or made Christ's.

41 **What is the outward and visible sign in Baptism?**
The outward and visible sign in Baptism is water in which the person is baptized *In the Name of the Father, and of the Son, and of the Holy Ghost.*

42 **What is the inward and spiritual gift in Baptism?**
The inward and spiritual gift in Baptism is union with Christ in his death and resurrection, the forgiveness of sins, and a new birth into God's family, the Church.

43 **What is required of persons to be baptized?**
It is required that persons to be baptized should turn from sin, believe the Christian Faith, and give themselves to Christ to be his servants.

44 **Why then are infants baptized?**
Infants are baptized because, though they are not yet old enough to make the promises for themselves, others, making the promises for them, can claim their adoption as children of God.

45 **What is *Confirmation*?**
Confirmation is the ministry by which, through prayer with the laying on of hands by the Bishop, the Holy Spirit is received to complete what he began in Baptism, and to give strength for the Christian life.

46 **What is required of persons to be confirmed?**
It is required that persons to be confirmed should have been baptized, be sufficiently instructed in the Christian Faith, be penitent for their sins, and be ready to confess Jesus Christ as Saviour and obey him as Lord.

47 **What is *Holy Communion*?**
Holy Communion is the Sacrament in which, according to Christ's command, we make continual remembrance of him, his passion, death, and resurrection, until his coming

again, and in which we thankfully receive the benefits of his sacrifice.

It is, therefore, called the Eucharist, the Church's sacrifice of praise and thanksgiving; and also the Lord's Supper, the meal of fellowship which unites us to Christ and to the whole Church.

48 **What is the outward and visible sign in Holy Communion?**
The outward and visible sign in Holy Communion is bread and wine given and received as the Lord commanded.

49 **What is the inward and spiritual gift in Holy Communion?**
The inward and spiritual gift in Holy Communion is the Body and Blood of Christ, truly and indeed given by him and received by the faithful.

50 **What is meant by receiving the Body and Blood of Christ?**
Receiving the Body and Blood of Christ means receiving the life of Christ himself, who was crucified and rose again, and is now alive for evermore.

51 **What are the benefits we receive in Holy Communion?**
The benefits we receive are the strengthening of our union with Christ and his Church, the forgiveness of our sins, and the nourishing of ourselves for eternal life.

52 **What is required of those who come to Holy Communion?**
It is required of those who come to Holy Communion that they have a living faith in God's mercy through Christ, with a thankful remembrance of his death and resurrection; that they repent truly of their sins, intending to lead the new life; and be in charity with all men.

53 **What is *Ordination*?**
Ordination is the ministry in which, through prayer with the laying on of hands, our Lord Jesus Christ gives the grace of the Holy Spirit, and authority, to those who are being made bishops, priests, and deacons.

54 **What is *Holy Matrimony*?**
Holy Matrimony is Christian marriage, in which the man and the woman, entering into a life-long union, take their vows before God and seek his grace and blessing to fulfil them.

55 **What is the ministry of *Absolution*?**
The ministry of absolution is the ministry by which those who are truly sorry for their sins, and have made free confession of them to God in the presence of the minister, with intention to amend their lives, receive through him the forgiveness of God.

56 **What is the sacramental ministry of *Healing*?**
The sacramental ministry of healing is the ministry by which God's grace is given for the healing of spirit, mind, and body, in response to faith and prayer, by the laying on of hands, or by anointing with oil.

VI. THE CHRISTIAN HOPE

57 **What is the hope in which a Christian lives?**
A Christian lives in the certain hope of the advent of Christ, the last judgement, and resurrection to life everlasting.

58 **What are we to understand by the advent of Christ?**
By the advent of Christ we are to understand that God, who through Christ has created and redeemed all things, will also through Christ at his coming again, make all things perfect and complete in his eternal kingdom.

59 **What are we to understand by the last judgement?**
By the last judgement we are to understand that all men will give account of their lives to God, who will condemn and destroy all that is evil, and bring his servants into the joy of their Lord.

60 **What are we to understand by resurrection?**
By resurrection we are to understand that God, who has overcome death by the resurrection of Christ, will raise from death in a body of glory all who are Christ's, that they may live with him in the fellowship of the saints.

61 **What, then, is our assurance as Christians?**
Our assurance as Christians is that neither death, nor life, nor things present, nor things to come, shall be able to separate us from the love of God which is in Christ Jesus our Lord. Thus, daily increasing in God's Holy Spirit, and following the example of our Saviour Christ, we shall at the last be made like unto him, for we shall see him as he is.

Therefore I pray:

May the God of all grace, who has called us unto his eternal glory by Christ Jesus, after that we have suffered awhile, make us perfect, stablish, strengthen, settle us.
To him be glory and dominion for ever and ever.
Amen.